Fin Has a Map

By Cameron Macintosh

Fin has a map.

Fin taps at a bit
of the map.

Fin can see a cat.

Fin sat to pat the cat.

The cat bit the map!

Fin ran at the cat!

The map!

Rip, rip, rip!

Fin can see sap!

Fin taps at the sap.

He taps at the map.

Tap, tap, tap!

CHECKING FOR MEANING

1. What did the cat do to the map? *(Literal)*

2. What did Fin do when he saw the cat running away? *(Literal)*

3. How did Fin fix his map? *(Inferential)*

EXTENDING VOCABULARY

pat	What does *pat* mean? Give an example of a sentence using the word *pat*.
ran	Look at the word *ran*. What smaller word is at the end of *ran*?
sap	What is *sap*? Which words do you know that describe *sap*?

MOVING BEYOND THE TEXT

1. Why did Fin need a map?

2. How do you think Fin felt when the cat bit his map? Why?

3. What could Fin do to prevent the cat from taking his map again?

4. Can you think of a time when you lost something important? How did you feel?

SPEED SOUNDS

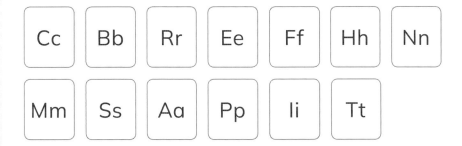

| Cc | Bb | Rr | Ee | Ff | Hh | Nn |

| Mm | Ss | Aa | Pp | Ii | Tt |

PRACTICE WORDS

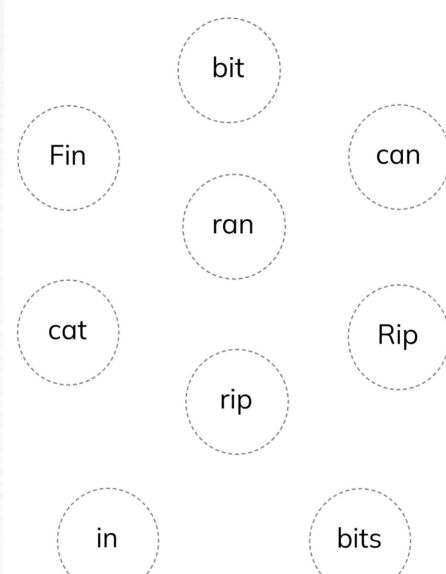

bit

Fin

can

ran

cat

Rip

rip

in

bits